Merry Christmas,
Carol
1970
When you need a lift, read
a couple poems!

UNICEF Book of CHILDREN'S
POEMS

UNICEF Book

of
CHILDREN'S
POEMS

compiled and with photographs
by *William I. Kaufman*

Adapted for English-reading children by
JOAN GILBERT VAN POZNAK

STACKPOLE BOOKS

Because the language of a child's
heart is universal, the photographs and poems have been arranged
to complement each other, according
to the meaning and feeling of each, rather
than by the country from which each comes.

And, in adapting these poems from
many lands for the English-reading
young person, their original form
and feel have been preserved. Where a
poem in its native land and language is
in rhyme, there has been a faithful effort to
keep its meaning and style in a rhyme form.
Nonsense words and animal sounds are re-
tained just as the children say them in their native
tongue in order to convey the beauty of sound and
rhythm of these poems in their original languages.

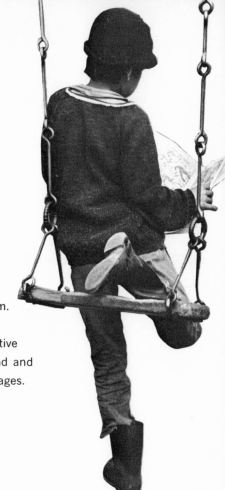

UNICEF BOOK OF CHILDREN'S POEMS

Copyright © 1970 by William I. Kaufman

Published by
    STACKPOLE BOOKS
    Cameron and Kelker Streets, Harrisburg, Pa. 17105, U.S.A.

Library of Congress Catalog Card Number 70-110476
ISBN 0-8117-1807-7
Printed in U.S.A.

Contents

Give me a lemon,
Give me a lime,
Give me your heart,
And I'll give you a rhyme.

Lemons and limes, butterflies and flowers, nightingales and doves are some of the beautiful gifts of nature that you read about in these poems. For centuries poets of every country have written about the gentility of the animals and the sweet smell of blossoms that grow on the hills and beside the smoothly flowing streams. They have given us sad poems about little lost lambs and happy poems about naughty little boys and girls.

As you read you may be surprised to discover that these poems express many feelings and thoughts that you have had yourself. They are the feelings and thoughts you share with the boys and girls who live in the distant lands from which these poems come. From Yugoslavia there is "Catch Me the Moon, Daddy," and from Venezuela "Look at the Moon," while from Iran the poetry speaks about butterflies and from Hong Kong about dragonflies. When you think about these poems you have an opportunity to consider how alike all children of the world are in the things which cause them to wonder and to question.

I know that wishing and dreaming are favorite pastimes for all boys and girls and while you are enjoying these poems you might imagine that you are in Thailand imitating the "Black Crow" or that you are in Korea riding on your "Bamboo Cane Companion."

Beauty is all around you and I hope that your heart is so happy that you are able to open your eyes wide to see and be thankful for all the gifts of nature that bring you joy and make you silly or serious, loving or devilish, gay or pensive.

Even though your wide-open eyes will also see much sadness, I pray that the understanding you get from these poems will help your heart to sing out as strongly as the heart of the black crow . . .

Look my child, can you see
What the good crow shows you and me?
Love and share your things together
And happiness is yours forever.

WILLIAM I. KAUFMAN

Photo: Hong Kong

Dragonfly

Dragonfly, Dragonfly,
Come over the river by and by;
On the eastern bank they are
beating a drum,
On the western bank they are striking
a gong.

Chinese, from Hong Kong

8

A New Game

Round and round, hand in hand,
dressed for a party,
we are going to play a new game in
the gay patio of my small country school . . .

Let all children come,
all races, all tongues, all colors.
Come from the coast, the mountains, the country,
the city, from every town . . .

Because children share one sweet word
their weeping is one, their smile too
because there is only one language for children . . .
Children speak to each other with the heart!

Let the little Negro come; he of the milk-white teeth,
of the tiny curls, of the coal-black skin.
There is a place in the circle knit with kisses
for the Congolese, for the Sudanese . . .
The little Chinese of the small feet,
Of the saffron skin, with the almond eyes.
Let him come into the circle made of children,
made of children of every color.

Let the little blonde snow-children come,
with the little blue eyes, skin white as fleece;
children who live on the banks of the Seine,
who drink the waters of the Rhine and the Don . . .

Let the little dark clay Indians come
of the pitch-black braids, of budding lips,
Indians who live on mountains and in valleys,
who grace the streets of Imperial Cuzco . . .

In my circle let songs be sung
in Chinese, Armenian, Russian and English;
in Quechua, Polish, Greek and French
let the children of the world say "brother."

Let them come wearing feathered headdresses,
silk kimonos, indigo turbans,
ponchos, caftans and saris
and parkas of gray caribou fur . . .

Leaving hut, cabin, tent and igloo,
let them come from the Pole, from Arabia,
let them come by air, by land and by sea . . .

Photo: Brazil

Not clothes, nor language, nor color, nor nation
can change the soul of the child;
in kissing, in crying and in song
the children of the world are one . . .

Luchi Blanco de Cuzco

Peru

AFSANA-SISANA

Afsana-Sisana
Forty birds clamor . . .
I cooked a very good stew
And ate it so nobody knew.
I gave some to a farmer to eat;
The farmer gave me some wheat.
I took the wheat to a mill;
They gave me flour, my fill.
With flour to a taghaar* I went;
The taghaar gave me some ferment.
The ferment I gave to a baker;
He gave me a loaf, the bread-maker.
To a shepherd I gave the bread;
He gave me a lamb instead.
The lamb to a wise man I took;
The wise man gave me a book.
The book I learned to read.
God has given me what I need.   Afghanistan

* A taghaar is one who prepares yeast for bread.

The

Oh my brothers, the rain has come.

Come, sit beneath the trees.

There are flowers; I'll give you some.

Here is fruit . . . eat these.

Breathe deeply . . . hear the raindrops drum.

Play no more; the rain has come.

Algeria

Rain Has Come

The Little Black Girl

All dressed in white,
starched and neat,
the little black girl stood
in the doorway of her house,
a stiff white ribbon
in her hair,
necklaces of red beads
circled her neck.

The other little girls
played in the street.
The other little girls
never played with her.

All dressed in white,
starched and neat,
in a silence without tears
the little black girl cried.

All dressed in white,
starched and neat,
the little black girl lies
in her pine coffin.

A white angel carries her
to the presence of God.
The little black girl doesn't know
if she should be happy or sad.

God looks at her sweetly.
He strokes her head
and attaches a lovely pair
of white wings to her back.
God smiles at the little black girl
and calls all the angels;
"Play with her," he tells them.

Colombia

Photo: Ecuador

Wonder, wonder,
  what can it be?
Its tracks can't be seen
  on sandy ground
Although in straw
  they can be found.

(the signs of a fire when a field is burned)

L e S

Wonder, wonder,
what can it be?
Thrown on a rock,
it will not shatter
But in water
it will tatter.

(paper)

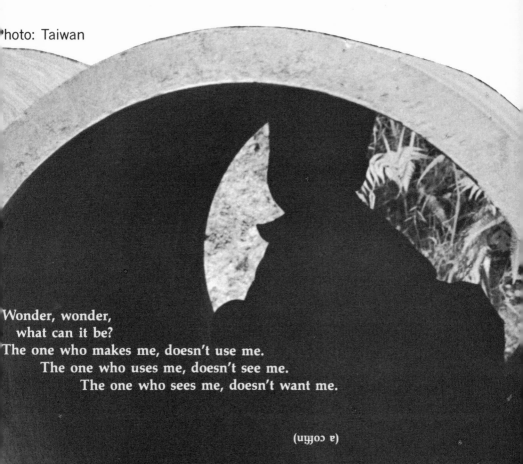

Photo: Taiwan

Wonder, wonder,
what can it be?
The one who makes me, doesn't use me.
The one who uses me, doesn't see me.
The one who sees me, doesn't want me.

(a coffin)

Paraguay

Snow

The tinsel snow flakes dancing in air

Spread a white velvet carpet everywhere;

Under the weight of the glittering snow

The branches of fir trees bent down low.

Inside a fire glowed warm and bright,

And we talked of snow by the fire-light;

How it melts and causes the streams to flow

And that in turn makes green things grow.

Then Mother said, "Bed-time, little one,

It will all be gone with tomorrow's sun."

Iran

Photo: Philippines

the Hummingbird

Prince of the garden!

For you the roses
Dress themselves in crimson robes.

Hummingbird.

You kiss them all and to all
You pledge your heart.

Flowerwooer.

But they all know that you
Will never marry. Bachelor!

Fernando Lujan

Costa Rica

Photo: Japan

FOLK

Photo: Nepal

*N*epal is a pleasant country.

The bright sun shines on peaks of snow;

Rhododendron blossoms in the mountains

And Kaas* in the river valleys below.

*Kaas is a flower.

POEM

The Daphe† and Munal‡ birds dance on the mountains.

Oh, ducks of the snow peaks, take me on your flights

To see the small villages scattered on hillsides,

To savor our motherland's many delights.

Nepal

†The Daphe is the national bird of Nepal, a beautiful rainbow-hued bird.
‡The Munal is a songbird.

Look at the Moon

Look at the moon
Singing a tune.
Look at the sun
Chewing a bun.
Look at the Virgin;
Upon my word,
She's washing the diapers
Of Our Lord!
Give me a lemon,
Give me a lime,
Give me your heart,
And I'll give you a rhyme.

Venezuela

Photo: Guatemala

Juan Volatin

In the cottage the children
In the ink-black night
Begin their vigil,
Desolate, quiet.
Crickets and birds
Heavy with sleep,
Flowers and clover
In darkness deep.

Anxious and mute,
The children sense
Terror, as howling
Dogs commence.

The desolate valley
They see, afraid,
And hear a sound
Though none is made.

Juan Volatin fell from the window.
Juan Volatin rolled over the pillow.
Juan Volatin, the goblin of night,
Begins his irritating bellow.

The good nymph comes
To the children, hovers,
Puts them to sleep
Under gentle covers.
She shows them scenes
Of smiling worlds, lifting
Their dreams where mysterious
Clouds are drifting.

Photo: Peru

*T*hen suddenly huge
Insects throng
Over Juan Volatin,
Dinning loud and long.
And soon they're stinging
Him, through his clothes,
His neck, his back;
Down, down he goes.

   *J*uan Volatin surrenders his cloak,
   Juan Volatin surrenders his sword,
   Juan Volatin rolls on the ground,
   Rolls over and over with never a word.

Peru

Cu cu, cu cu
Sang the frog
In the water.
A knight went by
With cloak and dagger.
A lady went by
With a train and a swagger.
A maid went by
On her way to the dairy.
A sailor went by,
Selling rosemary.
I asked for a bunch
But to no avail;
So full of rage
I began to wail.

Ecuador

Song of Fire

Fire that men watch in the night,
        In the deep night,
Fire that burns and does not warm, that sparkles
        And does not burn,
Fire that flies without substance, without heart, which
        Does not know either hut or home,
Fire of the palms, transparent, a fearless
        Man calls upon you.
Fire of the witches, where is your Father? Where
        Is your Mother? Who nursed you?
You are your father, you are your mother, you
        Pass through life and leave no remains.
Dry wood does not give you birth, you have no
        Ashes for daughters, you die and
        Do not die.
The wandering soul becomes transformed in you, and no one
        Knows it.
Fire of the witches, Spirit of the waters below,
        Spirit of the air above,
Ray that shines, firefly that lights
        The marshes,
Bird without wings, thing without substance,
        Spirit of the Strength of Fire,
Hear my voice: a fearless man
        Calls upon you.
    L. S. Senghor

                Senegal

oto: Ethiopia

TONGUE-TWISTER
IN
KIKAMBA

Nganganga ngungani

nguu siya

nganga

ngimantha

nganga

nga nguu.

which means:

I am wandering into an old cave
full of fungus,
to look for an old female guinea fowl.

Elizabeth Muoki [*]
Kenya

*Mrs. Muoki belongs to the Akamba tribe
and does her writing in English, using
the traditional folk literature of her
people in the Kibamba language
as the basis for her work.

Little Child

Child, little child,
How little you know.
Hasten to learn
As you hasten to grow.
The knowledge that
You now attain
Will never have been
Learned in vain.
It helps to earn
A livelihood,
Achieving much in life
That's good.
So come, give study a fair trial.
I promise it will be worthwhile.
Today bear with a little sorrow
So you'll be wise and smart tomorrow.

Thailand

Photo: Singapore

Are you a little angel
Delicate and soft,
Resting on a flower,
Fluttering aloft?

When Springtime is the season
And grass grows from the earth,
The brightly colored flowers
Are twinkling with mirth.

Butter

You waft into the garden
On the morning breeze,
Asking for the flowers,
Floating with such ease.

Birds are storytelling
As you find your way
On the leafy carpet;
You dance away the day.

So fragile and so lovely,
Ornate and pretty thing,
You're better than an angel.
Are you the child of Spring?

M. Kiyanoush   Iran

Photo: Japan

The little girls
of the cornfield
hang out their
saffron hair
in the sun
to dry.

The Little Girls

Dressed in fresh green,
on tiptoe they peek out
through the stalks in the wind.

Redheaded, tousled,
they smell of childhood
and of the earth just plowed.

Mother breeze pins on
tight hoods
so that their hair won't disarrange.

And still in the wind they toss
—promises of love and bread—
rebellious red locks!

Ester Feliciano Mendoza

f the Cornfield

Guatemala

TOTO is a little puppy

With a lot of shaggy hair

So that when he plays about,

Lots of dust gets in the air.

ALL around the house he muddies

But he's such a little dear;

Though I want to spank him hard,

His tail waggles when I'm near.

I am very fond of Toto.

Too bad he's got all those fleas,

And when I give him his dinner,

He wants seconds, if you please!

Heloisa Ramalho
(written at age 11)

Brazil

Photo: Morocco

THE
FOUR
SEASONS

"Oh, my eyes opened in awe.
I saw ... I saw ... I saw ..."
"Hush, don't shout so loudly, son.
What did you see, you naughty one?"
"Blossoms sprouting from the trees,
Birds flying in a soothing breeze,
The melted snow, streams overflow ...
So beautiful you cannot know!"

"Oh, my eyes opened in awe.
I saw ... I saw ... I saw ..."
"Hush, don't shout so loudly, son.
What did you see, you naughty one?"
"I saw green corn turned gold and sweet,
The mill full to the brim with wheat ...
Oh, how marvelous to see it!"

"Oh, my eyes opened in awe.
I saw ... I saw ... I saw ..."
"Hush, don't shout so loudly, son.
What did you see, you naughty one?"
"In the vineyards grapes I found.
Yellow leaves are on the ground;
Rain made the river overflow
And fog hangs in the valley low.
How wonderful to see it so!"

Photo: Indonesia

"Oh, my eyes opened in awe.
I saw . . . I saw . . . I saw . . ."
"Hush, don't shout so loudly, son.
What did you see, you naughty one?"
"I saw the sun, but wasn't warm,
The hills were white after the storm . . .
Oh, mama, guess what I have found?
I love my home the whole year round."

Turkey

CATCH ME THE MOON, DADDY

Catch me the moon, Daddy,
Let it shine near me awhile,
Catch me the moon, Daddy,
I want to touch its smile.

The moon must shine from high above;
That's where it needs to stay
Among the stars, to guide them home
When they return from play.

So the bunny can find his supper,
So the mouse can scamper free,
So the hedgehog can make his forays,
So the birds can sleep in the tree.

And as for you, my child,
With slender silver thread
The moon will weave sweet dreams, so you
May slumber in your bed.

Griger Vitez

Yugoslavia

Photo: Nepal

Poncho

Poncho, as Indian as my race,

Made with pure wool of the llama,

Bullfighter's cape of the strong wind,

You are my proud banner

raised above the mountain,

I am your topmast, triumphant, alive.

Oscar Alfara Gonzales

Bolivia

Photo: Colombia

Wedding of the Flowers

The pomegranate's daughter,
And the peony's favorite son,
    Have curtains made of jasmine,
And blankets of lilies spun,
    A couch of cinnamon flowers,
Pillows with snowball laden—
    Making a "hush, hush" sound.
Autumn Fragrance Maiden
    Steps in to sweep around;
And Maid of the Poppy Queen
    Comes into the bridal room;
She steps to the bower screen.
    With scent of silver flowers
Clinging to her face,
    And with lotus petals fragrant
On her lips—a trace,
    She walks a step apace:
Scent of a thousand flowers sows;
    She walks another step,
Shedding the dew of the rose;
    She walks another step,
And into the garden goes,
    Where balsam, lily, lotus,
Stand rows on rows.

Chinese, from Hong Kong

Photo: Singapor

This little finger
found a little egg,

This Little Finger

This little finger cooked it,

Photo: Brazil

And this
mischievous
fat one
ate it!

This little finger sprinkled
salt on it,

This little finger
scrambled it,

Costa Rica

WE ARE THE Happy

We are the happy world;
Within our world are songs
And stories of the
     glorious age
To which our world belongs.

From all the branches
     of the trees
Birds envy us our melodies
And to the flowers
     they fly and fuss,
Asking what they think of us.

World

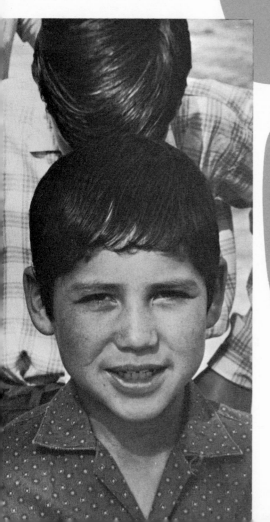

From Lebanon's paradise
   we come
Glowing with youth's bloom.
Our hearts are filled with joy
As we inhale the trees' perfume.

Born free, we cherish
   our beliefs,
We children of the flowers;
To love our neighbor
   and our guest—
These principles are towers.

Lebanon

Photo: Chile

55

Haiku

In the
    ancient pond
        I hear the
            sound of water.
                A little frog jumps.

In the
    gentle night
        Shrill chirrups
          of cicadas
            Pierce even
                through rock.

             Japan

            Photo: Japan

DING DONG, LITTLE BELLS OF ST. JOHN

Ding dong,
Little bells of St. John.
The rich eat cheese and bread
And those who need
They get none.
Ding dong,
How will they be fed?

Ding dong,
The little bells cry.
The rich eat cheese and bread
And all the rest
They will die.
Ding dong,
Who will bury the dead?

Ecuador

Photo: Colombia

Jacinta

the Monkey

Jacinta the monkey
wears ribbons of green.
She combs out her hair
and wants to be queen.

But the poor little monkey
has not got a crown.
She has only a prison
of figleaves brown.

A lawless parrot
sells her a dress,
a cloak of feathers,
a foam necklace.

Seeing herself
in a silver spring,
she cries with joy,
"What a beautiful thing!"

She builds a castle
with just one brick
surrounded with flowers,
a frog and a chick.

The monkey cooks
with milk and flour,
hangs out the clothes
on the castle tower.

Her monkey daughters
play all alone.
Her monkey husband
sits on the throne.

Maria Elena Walsh

Argentina

Photo: El Salvador

THE

In the hollow of a mountain tree
A little bird has made its morning nest,
And so the tree awakens with a heart
Embracing music deep within its breast.

NEST

When the sweet bird comes out of the hollow
To drink the fragrance, or to sip the dew,
The tree upon the mountain makes me feel
As if its heart has come out singing, too.

El Salvador

Photo: Pakistan

The Husband

What a handsome soldier
Marching very straight,
His gun upon his shoulder,
Guarding at the gate.

"Tell me, Mr. Soldier,
Have you been to war?"
"Yes, Ma'am, I have just returned.
What do you ask me for?"

"Have you seen my husband,
He's now been gone a year?"
"No, Ma'am, I don't think so,
But how did he appear?"

"He's very tall and slender
And wears a shiny hat.
He rides upon a Moorish horse . . .
A Frenchman gave him that."

"Yes, Ma'am, indeed I saw him.
He died last year, and he
Has written in his final will
That you should marry me."

"Good Lord! Oh, Heaven help me,
St. Inez send advice . . .
One husband was enough for me,
Why must I marry twice?"

Costa Rica

64

Description

Photo: Nepal

A white dove
Descended from the sky,
In his beak a branch
And on the branch a flower.
And he gave the flower
To a dark little girl.
You are worthier, my dusky child,
Than all the rays of the sun.

White Dove

Costa Rica

Photo: Senegal

Bon Voyage

With one half of a newspaper
I made a little boat,
And in the fountain of my home
It's nice to see it float.

My sister with her paper fan
Blows and blows on it.
Bon Voyage! Bon Voyage!
Little paper ship.

Mexico

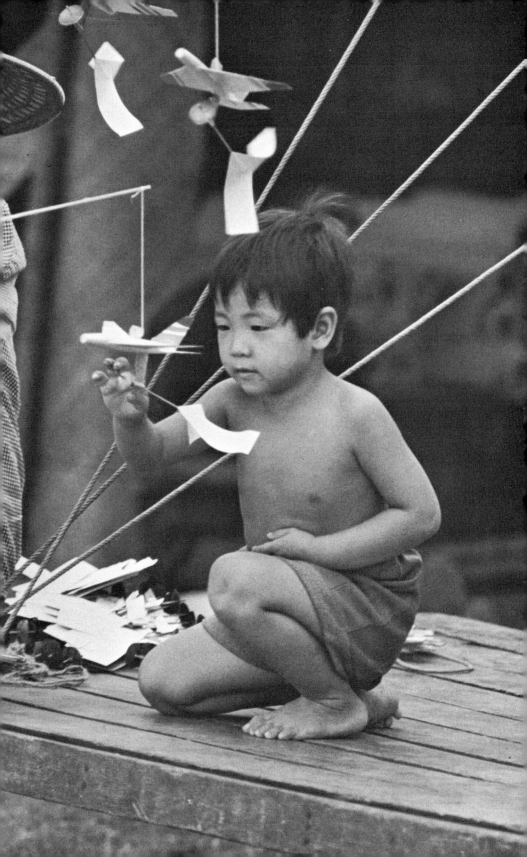

POEM
TO
MOTHERS

In your arms, Mother, in your arms
I will sleep sweetly.
I will sleep like the wind in the palm trees,
like the sky in the sea.

Your kisses will fall on my lips
when I sleep, when I sleep.
I will dream of the foam of the waves
caressing the sea.

Your words will be in my ears
a gentle lulling in my sleep;
I will dream with the wind
    and the breeze
singing to the sea.

Your clear eyes look into mine
with a sweet look
and I'll dream of the moon
    and the stars
shining on the sea.

In your arms, Mother, in your arms
I will learn to dream.

Mexico

Photo: Ghana

The Lio

There was a lion . . .

What kind of lion?

Very ferocious,

Grim and atrocious.

How terrible, how terrible!

Don't ask what he ate—

If he liked it . . . too late!

A tram and a track,

A cloud for a snack.

How terrible, how terrible!

He stepped with three legs,
He watched with three eyes,
He listened with three ears.
How terrible, how terrible!

Sharp teeth, evil eye,
He'd pass nothing by.
How terrible, how terrible!

Brana one day
Rubbed him away
With his eraser.
How terrible, how terrible!

Dusan Radovic

Yugoslavia
Photo: Japan

Shy Sea Shell

I found a shell on the beach one day
Half-buried in the sand;
I scooped it out from where it lay
And held it in my hand.

"Dear shell," said I, "I wonder why
You left your home at sea."
The shell then seemed to heave a sigh,
Yet would not answer me.

"Where are your playmates of the deep—
The ones so dear to you?
Are there not special friends you keep
Out in the sea so blue?"

The shy sea shell lay in my hand
And would not answer me.
Perhaps it longed to be in sand
Deep in the cold, blue sea.

C. V. Ty

Philippines

Photo: Ghana

75

Nightingale Song

A nightingale perched on a branch
And sang her lovely song:
"Oh, my soul, my happy soul,
This is where I belong."

"I love the beauty of the Spring;
In nature there's no malice.
My life in treetops I prefer
To castle or to palace.

From rose tree to rose tree I fly;
My home's in branches young.
Just ask the breeze about my tunes
The roses have heard sung.

Oh, people mine, you must agree
I was born as you see me.
In cages there can be no joy;
If I am to sing, then free me!

photo: Hong Kong

Ma'rouf Al-Rusafi

Iraq

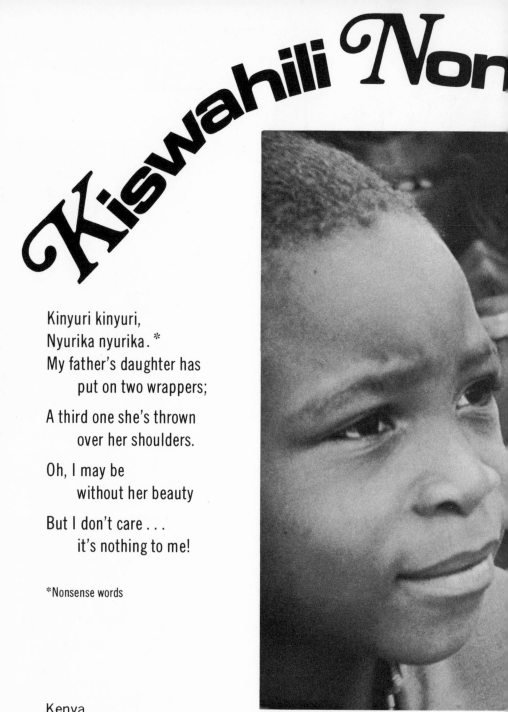

Kiswahili Non

Kinyuri kinyuri,
Nyurika nyurika.*
My father's daughter has
    put on two wrappers;

A third one she's thrown
    over her shoulders.

Oh, I may be
    without her beauty

But I don't care . . .
    it's nothing to me!

*Nonsense words

Kenya

sense Verse

Photo: Cameroon

The Good Black Crow
Loves his friends, you know.
In his wandering he will find
Food, and call out to his kind,
Inviting them to share his riches ...
Even a bite, but oh, it's delicious!

Look my child, can you see
What this good crow shows you and me?
Love and share your things together
And happiness is yours forever.

Thailand

Photo: Ceylo

Lullaby, naughty child,
Your nonsense
Drives your mama wild.

Lullaby, arrurru,
What can Mama
do with you?

Work all day,
Up all night,
By morning
nothing's
going right.

Lullaby, arrurru,
What can Mama do with you?

Venezuela

Photo: Nepal

Lullaby to a Naughty Baby

82

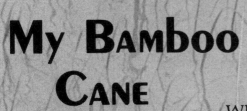

My Bamboo Cane Companion

When I see the bamboo cane,
I feel fond welcome as again
In childhood, happy and serene,
I rode my pony stick of green.
Now stands beside the window so,
Or walks with me if I would go.

Kim Kwang Wook

Korea

Photo: Korea

I am a little child
Clean as a little duck.
My ears are all washed,
My nails and hair are cut.

The whole day in school
With my bookbag
always near
I run, I play and jump
And I love my teacher dear.

Greece

am a little child*

*This poem was written by a student of the first grade at the Athena Lyceum in Amaroussion.

The Moon King's knife of silver bright

Floats over the waves on a quiet night,

Floats to the fiery Southern Sea

Where grows the giant Pepper Tree.*

When the pepper seeds to sea have gone,

The spring child sings his first little song.

*The Pepper Tree is, according to Chinese fairy lore, the largest in the universe. In autumn, when the pepper seeds are ripe, the baby who was born in early spring is able to sing a little.

Chinese, from Hong Kong

SILVER
KNIFE

There is

a little boy

There is a little boy.
His name is Jon.
When you say, "Go to school,"
He refuses utterly.
Says he: "I will stay home
To cut fruit from the palm tree."
Pufiki! Pufiki! His name is Jon.
Pufiki! Pufiki! His name is Jon.

the lost lamb

She walked so close, so close,
that she brushed me as I walked;
she wore a ribbon round her neck
and a metal bell . . .

She got lost as evening fell
in the shadows of the pine grove;
she wandered I don't know when.
I call her and she doesn't return.

Lambs from other flocks,
lambs from here and there
led her astray over paths,
some good, some bad, who knows.

I seem to see her,
and I run . . . but she's not there.
Her sleep-colored eyes,
where are they?

When the wood gets dark
and, weary of straying,
she returns looking
for the shepherd,
I will no longer be there.

I am the shepherd who does not wait
or who dies waiting!

Mexico

Photo: Guatemala

The
Four

There is a mother
With four children in all,
The Spring, the Summer,
The Winter and Fall.
Spring brings flowers,
Summer brings clover,
Fall offers grapes,
Winter, snow all over.
The heavens rejoice
And earth greets the day
When the favorite child,
Spring, is on its way.

Germany

Seasons

Photo: India

We are all men   Born as one,

Colored Brown, Black   **By the sun.**

For all men knowledge   Can be won,

But each man's heart   **Is his alone.**

Thailand

MAN'S HEART

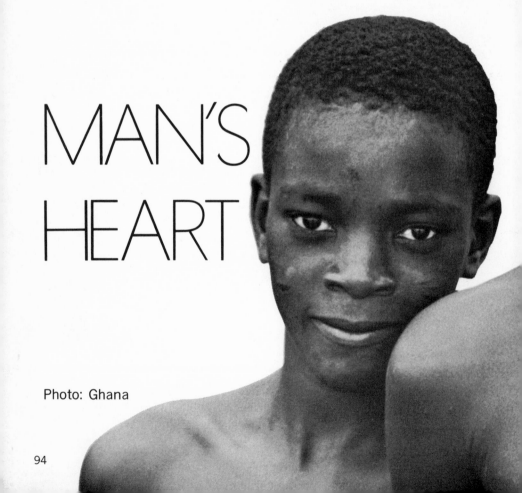

Photo: Ghana

94

ACKNOWLEDGMENT

I am indebted to so many for their help and cooperation that it would take a world almanac to include everyone by name who has made this vast project possible. To UNICEF in New York, Paris, and in each of the forty-two countries I visited I am especially grateful. To the ambassadors, ministers of education, ministers of culture and information, consular staffs and members of the staffs of the permanent missions to the United Nations, UNESCO staffs, religious leaders, translators, scholars, individual researchers, writers, parents and staffs of various welfare agencies for children who helped in the collecting of the written material, I say, "Bless you and thanks." I dream that all our efforts will help all our children to a greater understanding of each other.

WILLIAM I. KAUFMAN

about *William I. Kaufman*

WILLIAM I. KAUFMAN's love of children and belief that they are the hope of the world have led him to take on the almost impossible task of compiling material and photographing for this volume in forty-two countries. His over eighty books on a variety of subjects are published in English, French, German, Italian, Swedish, Japanese, Danish, Spanish and Arabic. Starting in the theater and continuing in television, he has pursued a successful creative life as a communications executive and consultant, a theatrical producer, a writer-editor, a teacher, a photographer and a song writer.

Design by Krone Art Serv